THE
NBA
A HISTORY OF HOOPS

Published by Creative Education
P.O. Box 227, Mankato, Minnesota 56002
Creative Education is an imprint of The Creative Company
www.thecreativecompany.us

Design and production by Christine Vanderbeek
Art direction by Rita Marshall

Printed by Corporate Graphics in the United States of America

Photographs by AP Images (Ed Kolenovsky, Gene Puskar),
Basketballphoto.com (Steve Lipofsky), Dreamstime (Munktcu), Getty
Images (Andrew D. Bernstein/NBAE, Lisa Blumenfeld, Jonathan
Ferrey, Focus on Sport, Sam Forencich/NBAE, Andy Hayt/Sports
Illustrated, Walter Iooss Jr./Sports Illustrated, Layne Murdoch/NBAE,
Joe Murphy/NBAE, Thomas Oliver/NBAE, Panoramic Images,
SM/AIUEO, Rocky Widner/NBAE), iStockphoto (Brandon Laufenberg)

Library of Congress Cataloging-in-Publication Data
LeBoutillier, Nate.
The story of the Portland Trail Blazers / by Nate LeBoutillier.
p. cm. — (The NBA: a history of hoops)
Includes index.
Summary: The history of the Portland Trail Blazers professional
basketball team from its start in 1970 to today, spotlighting the
franchise's greatest players and reliving its most dramatic moments.
ISBN 978-1-58341-959-5
1. Portland Trail Blazers (Basketball team)—History—Juvenile literature.
I. Title.
GV885.52.P67L43 2010   796.323'640979549—dc22   2009034787

GPSIA: 120109 PO1093

First Edition
2 4 6 8 9 7 5 3 1

Page 3: Guard Rudy Fernandez
Pages 4–5: Guard Steve Blake

THE STORY OF THE
PORTLAND
TRAIL BLAZERS

NATE LeBOUTILLIER

CREATIVE ◆ EDUCATION

CHAPTER ONE

A BLAZING BEGINNING

More than 200 years ago, explorers Meriwether Lewis and William Clark blazed a trail across the untamed American West. Their epic journey, which ended in the Pacific Northwest, opened the way for pioneers. In 1845, some of these pioneers set up a trading post that later became the city of Portland, Oregon. Today, the "City of Roses" and its metropolitan area is home to approximately two million people and is lauded for being one of the "greenest," or most environmentally friendly, cities in the United States.

In 1970, the National Basketball Association (NBA) decided to place a team in this growing city. Scores of fans responded to a "name the team" contest, and in the end, nearly 200 fans suggested some form of the name "Trail Blazers" in honor of the adventurous explorers who put Portland on the map. Although not all fans liked the name initially, it certainly was unique, as no professional or college sports team had

With its forests and rose gardens, and with majestic Mount Hood as a backdrop, the city of Portland is famous for its natural beauty.

ever used it previously. "It really wasn't very popular when fans first

heard it," Harry Glickman, executive vice president of the franchise, later

recalled. "But of course, we all know that changed."

Like most teams just starting out, the Trail Blazers lost a lot of games
their first few seasons. Even though Blazers fans saw few victories in
Portland's Memorial Coliseum, they were able to watch two special
players—sharpshooting guard Geoff Petrie and versatile forward Sidney
Wicks. Petrie was selected with the team's first pick in the 1970 NBA
Draft and quickly earned a reputation as a top outside marksman. Wicks,
meanwhile, was big enough to play center and quick enough to play
small forward, earning him the nickname "Mr. Everything."

As good as they were, Petrie and Wicks couldn't lead the Trail
Blazers to a winning record. But in the 1974 NBA Draft, Portland selected a 6-foot-11, redheaded center named Bill Walton. Walton could score
seemingly at will, yet he was also a great passer. Portland fans were

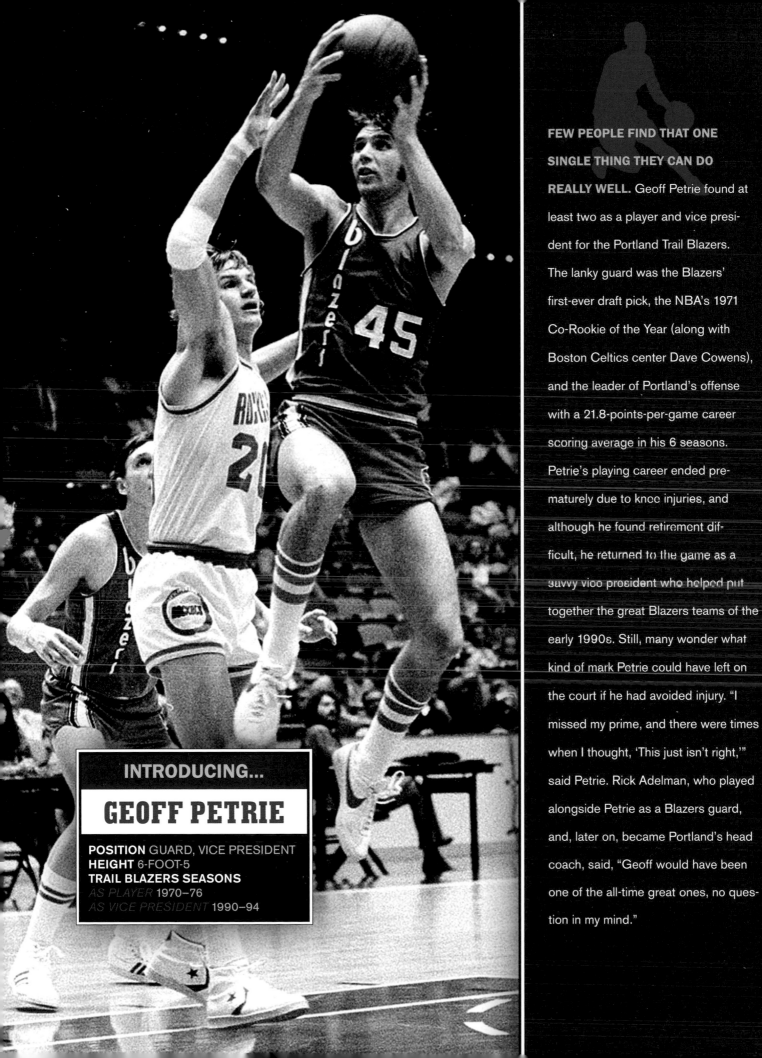

INTRODUCING...

GEOFF PETRIE

POSITION GUARD, VICE PRESIDENT
HEIGHT 6-FOOT-5
TRAIL BLAZERS SEASONS
AS PLAYER 1970–76
AS VICE PRESIDENT 1990–94

FEW PEOPLE FIND THAT ONE SINGLE THING THEY CAN DO REALLY WELL. Geoff Petrie found at least two as a player and vice president for the Portland Trail Blazers. The lanky guard was the Blazers' first-ever draft pick, the NBA's 1971 Co-Rookie of the Year (along with Boston Celtics center Dave Cowens), and the leader of Portland's offense with a 21.8-points-per-game career scoring average in his 6 seasons. Petrie's playing career ended prematurely due to knee injuries, and although he found retirement difficult, he returned to the game as a savvy vice president who helped put together the great Blazers teams of the early 1990s. Still, many wonder what kind of mark Petrie could have left on the court if he had avoided injury. "I missed my prime, and there were times when I thought, 'This just isn't right,'" said Petrie. Rick Adelman, who played alongside Petrie as a Blazers guard, and, later on, became Portland's head coach, said, "Geoff would have been one of the all-time great ones, no question in my mind."

FOR A PLAYER TO SCORE 50 POINTS IN A SINGLE NBA GAME IS A RARE FEAT—ONE THAT HAS BEEN ACHIEVED ONLY 4 TIMES IN TRAIL BLAZERS HISTORY. In January 1973, guard Geoff Petrie, renowned for his quick shooting release and pinpoint accuracy, tallied a career-high 51 points in a 130–115 win over the Houston Rockets. Two months later, Petrie again torched the nets (and the same Rockets) for another 51 in a 141–128 victory. In January 2005, pint-sized point guard Damon Stoudamire netted 54 points, which included 8 three-pointers, in a 112–106 loss to the New Orleans Hornets. "I was in a nice rhythm," said Stoudamire, "and even though I'm sitting here smiling and looking glad, I sure wish we would have had an inside scorer for a day. Then we could have a win." Stoudamire's 54 points topped Petrie's 32-year-old single-game Blazers record. "Thirty-some years is long enough," said Petrie. "It was a great performance, no doubt. My congratulations to Damon." In December 2008, young guard Brandon Roy joined Portland's elite fraternity with a 52-point effort in a 124–119 win over the Phoenix Suns.

COURTSIDE STORIES

THE 50-POINT CLUB

Damon Stoudamire shoots for two of his record-setting total in 2005.

disappointed when he didn't make the Blazers into winners in his first two seasons. The big center always seemed to have foot and ankle injuries, and "Blazermaniacs" wondered when things would change.

Portland hired a new coach named Jack Ramsay in 1976. Coach Ramsay demanded that Walton and other top players, such as guards Lionel Hollins and Dave Twardzik and forward Maurice Lucas, play aggressive defense and unselfish offense. No player did both better than Walton, who was finally healthy and able to play his best. "For two years, I wasn't able to run up and down the court freely without … thinking about [my injuries]," Walton explained. "That's no way to play basketball."

Behind their big center, the Trail Blazers made the playoffs for the first time after the 1976–77 season, then shocked the sports world by beating the Chicago Bulls, Denver Nuggets, and Los Angeles Lakers to reach the NBA Finals. In the Finals, the Trail Blazers faced the Philadelphia 76ers and their star swingman, Julius "Dr. J" Erving. The 76ers won the first two games in Philadelphia, sending the Blazers back home in a big hole. But a surprise awaited them. "When we got back to Portland after being down 0–2, there were 5,000 fans at the airport," Walton later recalled. "When we got off that plane and we saw the level of support and the level of commitment, there was no way we were ever going to give up."

AS A BASKETBALL ANNOUNCER FOLLOWING HIS PLAYING CAREER, BILL WALTON LOVED TO PREACH PEACE, LOVE, AND BASKETBALL. But those who remembered the aging hippie in his youth recalled occasional irritability and insubordination. "Off the floor I worried," remembered his college coach at the University of California, Los Angeles (UCLA), John Wooden.

"I worried when he was thrown in jail with the group that took over the administration building...and when he interrupted classes giving his views on the Vietnam War." Walton's NBA career was bittersweet. He won league championships with the Blazers in 1977 and with the Boston Celtics, in a limited role, in 1986. But in between, there were scores of debilitating injuries,

spats with journalists, and arguments with coaches and management. Walton made it through the ups and downs to become an announcer with a rosy outlook.

Forward Kevin McHale, a teammate in Boston, said, "You watch an old, old guy like that, with the most hammered body in sports, acting like a high school kid. It's both funny and inspiring at the same time."

Portland went into Game 3 with a little extra motivation, too. Although the Blazers had lost Game 2, Lucas and 76ers center Darryl Dawkins had gotten into a short but spectacular fight near the end of the game. Even though Dawkins was a powerful player, "Big Mo" proved that he was not intimidated. Inspired by Lucas's tenacity and their home crowd, the Blazers rebounded to win the next three games.

In Game 6 in Portland, the Blazers put on a clinic of defense and teamwork. With only seconds left and the Blazers ahead 109–107, Philadelphia forward George McGinnis drove to the basket and lofted up a shot that hit the front iron. Walton batted it back toward midcourt as the final seconds evaporated, the horn sounded, and fans rushed the court to celebrate. Walton tore off his jersey and launched it joyfully toward the rafters. "If I had caught the shirt, I would have eaten it," Lucas said. "Bill's my hero."

COURTSIDE STORIES

A FORTUITOUS FIGHT

Maurice Lucas squares off against Darryl Dawkins in the 1977 Finals.

DURING THE 1977 NBA FINALS, BASKETBALL BRIEFLY TURNED INTO BOXING. The star-laden 76ers were about to take a two-games-to-none series lead over the Trail Blazers when, late in Game 2, 76ers center Darryl Dawkins and Portland guard Bobby Gross tumbled roughly to the floor. Dawkins popped up and threw a wild swing at Gross, only to have slim but tough Blazers forward Maurice Lucas sprint up behind him and clock him. Chaos erupted as the two exchanged non-connecting punches, and players, fans, and security guards spilled onto the Philadelphia court. The fracas turned out to be the series' turning point. "I thought that changed how we felt about ourselves," said Lucas. "It changed their game for sure. It let them know that we were going to play them regardless of who they are and what they've done." Dawkins was so riled up following the game that he used his legendary strength to uproot and smash a locker room toilet. Those expecting further fisticuffs were disappointed when Lucas shook Dawkins's hand before the Game 3 tip-off. The Blazers won the next four games and the NBA title.

The next day, 150,000 people lined the streets of downtown Portland for a victory parade. "I'll never be able to think of that Monday without smiling," Glickman later said. "It was just such a great day for Portland and the whole state…. Everybody had signs that said, 'Rip City' or 'Red-Hot and Rollin'.'" Walton, too, would forever cherish the memory. "Team chemistry is what it's all about—the ability of five to think as one," he said. "That's what everybody on that great Blazer team did."

COURTSIDE STORIES

BLAZERMANIA

A Trail Blazers playoff rally.

DOWN TWO GAMES TO NONE TO THE 76ERS IN THE 1977 NBA FINALS, THE BLAZERS NEEDED A PICK-ME-UP. When they arrived home from Philadelphia after Game 2, they were greeted at the airport by thousands of Blazers supporters in a fanatical tizzy that came to be known as "Blazermania." As Bill Walton, center of that Portland team, said, "The Blazermaniacs fell in love with the team because of the way we played, the unselfishness, and the teamwork." Together in spirit, Blazers players and fans unleashed an inspired performance upon the 76ers in Game 3 for a decisive 129–107 Portland victory. The Blazers rolled to three straight victories from there on out to send Blazermania into overdrive. Local interest in the team briefly waned after the turn of the century, but signs of Blazermania reemerged when the team landed the 2007 NBA Draft's top pick, center Greg Oden. Season-ticket sales jumped, and Blazers home games became the place, again, for Portlanders to spend their winter nights. "You can tell right away," said former Blazers forward Maurice Lucas, "people are reengaged."

CHAPTER TWO

CLYDE GLIDES IN

Portland fans prepared for another championship parade when the Blazers opened 50–10 the next season. But Walton broke his foot in the first round of the playoffs, and the Blazers lost. A few months later, the star center—who felt that the Blazers medical staff had not treated his injury properly—stunned Portland by announcing that he wanted to be traded, a demand that the Blazers soon met, sending him to the San Diego Clippers.

Players such as center Mychal Thompson and guard Jim Paxson kept the Blazers competitive, but while they made the playoffs in the three seasons after Walton left town, they were no longer a championship contender. In 1981–82, the team missed the postseason despite a 42–40 record. A back injury that forced the retirement of forward Kermit Washington, Portland's leading rebounder and an NBA All-Defensive team selection the two previous seasons, didn't help matters.

Jim Paxson spent eight full seasons with the Blazers, steadily filling up the nets to become, by 1988, Portland's all-time leading scorer.

WIDELY REGARDED AS HAVING ONE OF THE SAGEST COACHING MINDS IN THE HISTORY OF THE NBA, DR. JACK RAMSAY LED THE BLAZERS TO THE LONE LEAGUE CHAMPION-SHIP IN THEIR HISTORY. Born in Pennsylvania, Ramsay was educated at Philadelphia's Saint Joseph's College and earned a doctorate in the field of education. He later coached for Saint Joseph's, and his successes there led him to the general manager's position with the Philadelphia 76ers and, eventually, on to Portland, where he guided the Blazers to the playoffs in 9 of his 10 seasons as coach. "The whole atmosphere in Portland was a huge psychological lift for me and the players," said Ramsay. "The fans … provided a constant din of support. For a coach, there couldn't have been a better environment." Ramsay, who valued selfless team play above all, enjoyed his finest hour when the Blazers won the 1977 title. "My favorite moment was in Game 6," Ramsay recalled, "when Bill Walton tapped a missed Sixers shot toward the backcourt and [guard] Johnny Davis ran it down as the clock expired. We were NBA champions."

INTRODUCING...

JACK RAMSAY

COACH
TRAIL BLAZERS SEASONS 1976–86

The 1982–83 season saw the Blazers climb back into the postseason, thanks to the maturation of forward Calvin Natt, who averaged 20.4 points per game, along with the wise coaching of Ramsay and steady play of Thompson in the post and Paxson on the perimeter. The team swept the Seattle SuperSonics in the first round of the Western Conference playoffs but fell to the mighty Lakers in the second round.

In the 1983 NBA Draft, the Blazers plucked 6-foot-7 shooting guard Clyde Drexler out of the University of Houston with the 14th overall pick. At first, many fans thought Drexler was just an average player with extraordinary jumping ability. He had a mediocre rookie season but played in every game and slowly improved. Drexler, nicknamed "Clyde the Glide" because of his smooth moves and impressive vertical leap, would soon show fans he could do it all.

The Blazers fell in the first round of the 1984 playoffs, and in the off-season, they decided to shake things up, trading several players to the Nuggets for forward Kiki Vandeweghe. Neither the fastest nor the most athletic player on the court, Vandeweghe instead used his intelligence to become a feared scorer. "[The defender] is always going to make a mistake—leaning the wrong way, too close, the wrong foot forward, shifting his eyes," he once explained. "You just have to wait for his mistake and capitalize on it."

n the 1984 NBA Draft, center Hakeem Olajuwon was selected first overall by the Houston Rockets, and the Trail Blazers, wanting to add size to their lineup, passed over a 6-foot-6 shooting guard named Michael Jordan and used the second pick to take 7-foot-1 center Sam Bowie. The Bulls snapped up Jordan, who went on to become, arguably, the greatest player in the history of basketball. "We wish [Jordan] were seven feet, but he's not," Bulls general manager Rod Thorn lamented after the Draft. "There just wasn't a center available. What can you do?"

Even though the Blazers already had the talented Drexler in the shooting guard slot, Portland fans would come to lament the decision to pass on Jordan. While Bowie wasn't a complete bust, averaging 10 points, 8.6 rebounds, and 2.7 blocks per game in his rookie season, he paled in comparison with Jordan, who netted 28.2 points per game and won the NBA's Rookie of the Year award. In addition to Bowie, the 1984 Draft also provided the Blazers with hard-nosed forward Jerome Kersey in the second round.

With Drexler's steady improvement, Vandeweghe's 22.4 points per outing, and the continued contributions of Thompson and Paxson, the 1984–85 Blazers were a formidable team. They stomped the Dallas

Mavericks in the playoffs but then lost, again, to the Lakers, who went
on to capture the NBA title. The following season, the team integrated
another talented rookie—point guard Terry Porter—into its system, but
Portland again made a swift exit from the playoffs. An era came to an
end after that season when rookie head coach Mike Schuler replaced
Jack Ramsay on the Blazers' bench.

Under Schuler, who was voted NBA Coach of the Year, the Blazers
became the NBA's highest-scoring team in 1986–87, putting up 117.9
points per game. Portland also made headlines that season by trading the aging Thompson to the Spurs for forward/center Steve Johnson
and swinging another trade for seven-foot center Kevin Duckworth.
Although the Blazers improved to 49–33, they fell in the playoffs' first
round. Portland raised its record again in 1987–88 to 53–29, but a
first-round postseason loss again ended any title aspirations.

IN COLLEGE, CLYDE DREXLER WAS A MEMBER

OF A HIGHFLYING, MADE-UP FRATERNITY AT THE

UNIVERSITY OF HOUSTON CALLED "PHI SLAMMA

JAMMA." When the Trail Blazers selected him with the
14th pick in the 1983 NBA Draft, he took his exciting
game to Portland. Soon, he was filling up the bucket
with his gliding dunks and driving lay-ins. As Portland

filled in talent around Drexler, the Blazers improved and
ultimately made it to the NBA Finals twice in the early
1990s. In the 1992 Finals, Drexler squared off against
Michael Jordan of the Chicago Bulls. Drexler and Jordan
were two of the most athletic shot-makers ever to take
the same court, and although Jordan's Bulls outlasted
Drexler's Blazers to win the title, both stars put on a

worthy show. Drexler went back home to Houston to finish his pro career with the Rockets, who won the 1995
NBA championship. "He was just the best athlete to
ever play in Portland," said Steve Jones, a former
Blazers forward. "He could make a way when there
was no way to be made."

CHAPTER THREE

A NEW DIRECTION

Multimillionaire Paul Allen bought the Trail Blazers in 1988, and other changes followed. Midway through the 1988–89 season, with the Blazers scuffling along at a mediocre 25–22, Allen fired Schuler and promoted assistant coach Rick Adelman. The new owner was widely criticized for firing such a successful coach. "I think it's a disgrace," former Utah Jazz coach Frank Layden said. "Mike is an excellent coach. Nobody works harder than he does. Definitely, the animals are running the zoo in Portland."

A popular Portland player soon bid farewell when the team parted ways with Vandeweghe in 1989, trading him to the New York Knicks. Coach Adelman's squad struggled to a 14–21 finish and then lost in the playoffs' first round for the fourth straight season. In the off-season, Portland made a low-post change, trading Bowie away for hardworking power forward

Kiki Vandeweghe had a knack for getting to the free-throw line and then cashing in; in 1985–86, he hit 523 shots from the "charity stripe."

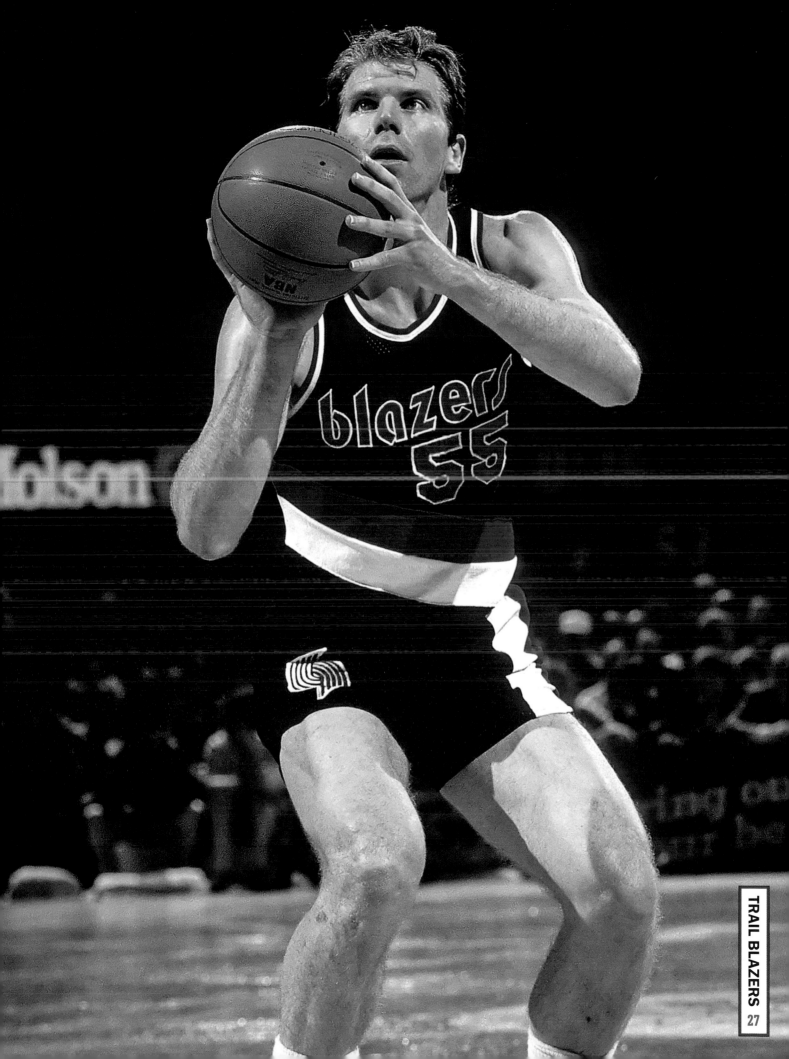

Buck Williams. Bowie left town having played just 139 out of a possible 410 games due to leg injuries over the course of his seemingly cursed Blazers career. "I'm not going to sit here and complain about the bad time I've had," said Bowie. "You see people who lose legs because of cancer, accidents. I'm not complaining." Although Bowie went on to play six more relatively healthy seasons in the NBA elsewhere, he never overcame the stigma of being selected before Jordan.

After all the personnel changes, Adelman knew that the 1989–90 Blazers had talent. Kersey, Duckworth, and Williams formed a burly inside combination, while Porter paired with Drexler to form a great outside attack. In addition, rookie forward Clifford Robinson proved to be a stellar pickup, averaging nearly 10 points a game and adding firepower off the bench. Portland improved its win total by 20 to finish the regular season 59–23. Suddenly, the Trail Blazers looked like a contender again.

SINCE 1988, THE TRAIL BLAZERS HAVE BEEN OWNED BY ONE OF THE RICHEST MEN IN THE WORLD: PAUL ALLEN. Allen's fortunes stem from 1975, when, along with Bill Gates, he cofounded the Microsoft Corporation. Today, the businessman and philanthropist owns a number of other entertainment and technology companies and has donated more than $1 billion to charitable causes. He has also earned a reputation as a sportsman, as he owns the Seattle Seahawks pro football team and is a minority owner of the Seattle Sounders, a Major League Soccer team that began play in 2009. Although Allen was always willing to open his wallet to better his teams, that free-spending strategy backfired in the mid-2000s when the Blazers paid bloated contracts to underperforming players on perennially underachieving Blazers squads. By 2009, Allen had reined in the spending and—with some lottery luck and shrewd decisions—rebuilt a winner. One of Allen's former players, Mark Bryant, a Trail Blazers forward from 1988 to 1995, described Allen as a regular guy. "The way he carried himself, you'd never know he owned the team," said Bryant. "People in Portland relate to that."

INTRODUCING...
PAUL ALLEN

TEAM OWNER
TRAIL BLAZERS SEASONS
1988–PRESENT

The Blazers fought their way through the 1990 playoffs, defeating the Dallas Mavericks, Spurs, and Suns to reach the NBA Finals, where they met the defending league champion Detroit Pistons. The Blazers won one of two games in Detroit but, uncharacteristically, lost the next three in Portland as the Pistons won out. True to form, a mob of Portland fans 7,000 strong nonetheless showed up for a hometown rally after the series to express their thanks and hopes for the future. "We had six new people on this team this year and we reached the NBA Finals," said Drexler. "I just think the future looks so bright."

The next year, Portland added veteran guard Danny Ainge and started the season 19–1. The Blazers finished with a 63–19 record, the best in team history, but lost to the Lakers in the Western Conference finals. The loss made Drexler and his teammates more determined than ever to finally get over the hump and win another NBA title for Portland. "We're a better team than we showed," Drexler said. "We'll be back."

Rugged forward Jerome Kersey played the best ball of his career in the 1990 playoffs, averaging 20.7 points and 8.3 rebounds per game.

CHAPTER FOUR

RUNNING WITH THE BULLS

D rexler shot and dunked his way to an average of 25 points per game in 1991–92 and helped Portland roll to a 57–25 record. In the postseason, the Blazers battled past three opponents to reach their second championship series in three seasons. Drexler and his teammates then faced one of the toughest teams of all time in the NBA Finals: the Chicago Bulls, led by the great Jordan.

The two teams split the first four games before the Bulls captured Game 5. Portland was up 17 points in the third quarter of Game 6 in Chicago, but the Bulls came roaring back. "Chicago's defensive intensity picked up, and we didn't handle the ball well," said Coach Adelman, who called five timeouts in the fourth quarter to try to compose his team. "Our guys just ran out of gas." The result was a 97–93 win, and an NBA title, for the Bulls.

Terry Porter's leadership at the point position helped make Portland nearly as powerful as three-time champion Chicago in the early '90s.

That was the last hurrah for the Blazers. A number of the team's top players were traded away over the course of the next few seasons, and Portland slipped in the standings. Many fans were saddened in 1995 when Drexler was traded to the Rockets, who promptly won the NBA championship. It seemed the exciting days in Rip City were over.

After Drexler's departure, the Blazers rebuilt around center Arvydas Sabonis. A 7-foot-3 giant from Lithuania who had played for many years in Europe, Sabonis was a skilled rebounder and shooter. He could also flip the ball behind his back or fire full-court passes with the feathery touch of a point guard. "Arvydas and Bill Walton are the two best passing big men ever," said then Milwaukee Bucks coach Mike Dunleavy. "No one else is even close."

Paul Allen, the Trail Blazers' wealthy owner, paid top dollar to surround Sabonis with talent. In the late '90s, Portland fans saw some exciting performances by such players as dynamic guard Isaiah Rider and fiery forward Rasheed Wallace. These players gave the Blazers the firepower to beat the NBA's best teams on any given night. But they were also prone to losing skids, and Rider, Wallace, and other

players often threw temper tantrums and behaved badly off the court.

In 1998–99, the Blazers seemed about ready to make another run at an NBA title. With zippy new point guard Damon Stoudamire running a fast-paced offense—and with 20,000 fans cheering them on in the new Rose Garden in downtown Portland every night—the Blazers streaked all the way to the Western Conference finals before losing to the Spurs. A few weeks after the loss, Portland traded for All-Star guard Scottie Pippen, who had helped the Bulls win six NBA championships.

With Pippen on board, the Blazers battled their way back to the conference finals in 2000 and a showdown with the Lakers. The Lakers, who were led by star center Shaquille O'Neal, jumped out to a three-games-to-one series lead, but the Blazers won

the next two. In the deciding Game 7, the Blazers had the Lakers on the
ropes, building a 15-point lead in the fourth quarter. But Portland fans
watched in pain and disbelief as the Lakers stormed back for the win.
"It's tough to swallow right now," Pippen said sadly after the game, "and
I'm sure it will be all summer."

Scottie Pippen and the Blazers found their 2000 conference finals collapse even more bitter after the Lakers went on to win the NBA title.

ONE OF THE SORRIEST SITUATIONS PORTLAND BASKETBALL FANS EVER HAD TO ENDURE WAS THE END OF CLYDE DREXLER'S BLAZERS CAREER. Over the span of 11 and a half seasons, Drexler became arguably the best guard in team history. But going into his 12th season in black and red, he was just the eighth-highest paid player on the team, and he was upset over trade rumors involving him. Halfway through the 1994–95 season, with the Blazers 25–20 and Drexler averaging a team-high 22 points per game, relations between "The Glide" and the team became so acrimonious that Drexler made a public demand for a trade, saying, "I want to get out. Anything that means leaving here will make me happy." The Blazers acquiesced, trading Drexler to the Rockets for power forward Otis Thorpe. Drexler won the NBA championship with Houston that season, while the Blazers were swept out of the playoffs' opening round by the Suns. Said Blazers point guard Terry Porter at the time of the trade: "Clyde Drexler was the identity of the Portland Trail Blazers, and there will be no substitute."

CHAPTER FIVE

A FRESH TRAIL

The stunning collapse against the Lakers seemed to end the momentum that had been building in Portland, and the team made quick playoff exits the next few seasons. By 2004, the Blazers were a franchise with a new look. Gone were Pippen and Wallace, replaced by younger players such as forwards Zach Randolph and Shareef Abdur-Rahim. A 27–55 record (the team's worst in 32 years) in 2004–05 made it clear that Portland needed to rebuild once again.

The Blazers took a step in the right direction by hiring coach Nate McMillan in 2005. McMillan had spent 19 years playing and coaching in neighboring Seattle for the Super-Sonics, and he had built a reputation as a man who knew how to teach young players. Many fans were surprised Portland was able to lure him away from Seattle. McMillan explained his decision for the move simply. "There is a winning tradition here," he said upon arriving in the City of Roses. "That is part of the reason that I'm here. I want to try to bring that back to the community."

LaMarcus Aldridge joined the Blazers in 2006 via the team's old rival, the Bulls, who drafted the young forward and promptly traded him.

COURTSIDE STORIES

Portland forward Rasheed
Wallace objects to a referee's call.

THE JAIL BLAZERS

THE PEOPLE OF PORTLAND HAD CARRIED ON A LOVE AFFAIR WITH THEIR PROFESSIONAL BASKETBALL TEAM FROM ITS INCEPTION IN 1970 UP UNTIL THE MID-1990s. About half a million people live within Portland's city limits, making it one of the NBA's smallest markets, and for years, the small-town feeling meant a close-knit relationship between players and fans. But prior to the 1998–99 season, NBA owners locked out players because, in part, of player salaries that had escalated astronomically. The situation irritated fans, some of whom had begun to look upon modern NBA players as spoiled, greedy crybabies who thought they could get away with anything. The NBA and its players came to an agreement, but several Portland players who returned to work continued their wayward off-court behavior. Due to a number of player arrests, various sportswriters started calling Portland's team the "Jail Blazers," and the nickname caught on.

"The Jail Blazers were distasteful to [the point] where you didn't want to be associated with them," said forward Maurice Lucas, who played for Portland in the late 1970s. To Portland's credit, players considered bad apples were eventually jettisoned as the team rebuilt its roster and reputation.

McMillan and the Blazers struggled mightily in 2005–06, going 21–61. But through a trade on the day of the 2006 NBA Draft, Portland managed to land talented guard Brandon Roy, whose clutch shot-making and confident leadership helped him capture the league's 2007 Rookie of the Year award. After improving to 32–50, the Blazers overcame steep odds to win the 2007 Draft Lottery, then obtained coveted seven-foot center Greg Oden with the Draft's first pick. "The big man is the foundation, the man you build around," McMillan said.

Enthusiasm about Oden's arrival in Portland was soon tempered when it was found that the young center required knee surgery that would delay his appearance on the court for a year. Still, the Blazers continued to improve, thanks to Roy's steady play and the help of two veterans: point guard Steve Blake and Joel Przybilla, who filled the center spot admirably in Oden's place. Portland finished 41–41 in 2007–08.

The Blazers continued to add talent by trading for speedy guard Jerryd Bayless, the 11th overall pick of the 2008 NBA Draft. When Bayless joined a healthy Oden and talented forwards LaMarcus Aldridge, Nicolas Batum, and Rudy Fernandez on the revamped Blazers roster, the basketball party in Portland began anew. The Blazers went 54–28 and 50–32 the next two seasons before suffering first-round playoff defeats both times.

HUSTLEBOARD
BLAZERS GUEST
1 BLOCKED SHOTS 1
21 REBOUNDS 24
8 STEALS

BLAZERS
FANS
OUR 6TH MAN!

STATS CEN
BLAZERS GUEST BLAZ
48 FIELD GOAL PCT. 51 14
44 FREE THROW PCT. 66 21
4 FREE THROWS MADE 4 12
50 3 - POINT PCT. 14 6
4 3 - POINTERS MADE 1 2
3 OFF REBOUNDS 1 6
2 2ND CHANCE PTS. 2 14

HIGH SPEED INTERN

866 O.SA

COURTSIDE STORIES

STREAKS
OF SUCCESS

Center Joel Przybilla muscles his way to the rim for a score.

PORTLAND HAS ENJOYED ITS SHARE OF NBA HIGHLIGHTS SINCE JOINING THE LEAGUE IN 1970, CAPTURING ONE WORLD CHAMPIONSHIP, MAKING THREE NBA FINALS APPEARANCES, AND REACHING THE WESTERN CONFERENCE FINALS SIX TIMES. But perhaps most remarkable of all has been the Trail Blazers' consistency year after year as a formidable team. From 1976–77 to 2002–03, the Blazers made the playoffs every season but one—a staggering run of 26 playoff trips in 27 years, including 21 in a row. When the streak finally ended in 2004, then-coach Maurice Cheeks said, "I know there's a lot of disappointed people because we didn't make the playoffs. But my message to them is we have something special to build on." Cheeks wasn't around to experience it, but the Blazers finally made it back to the playoffs in 2009 and 2010 and seemed poised to get comfortable in the postseason again. Also impressive has been the Blazers' record of fan support. Between 1977 and 1995, "Rip City" fans put together an amazing 814-game sellout streak at Portland home games, the longest such streak in American professional sports.

INTRODUCING...

BRANDON ROY

POSITION GUARD
HEIGHT 6-FOOT-6
TRAIL BLAZERS SEASONS 2006–PRESENT

WHAT MAKES THE BEST BASKETBALL PLAYERS?

It's a simple question, but the answer can be hard to pinpoint. Certainly height is important, as is quickness, jumping ability, shooting touch, and ball-handling skill. But there is a sixth sense that some players, usually the best ones, possess that enables them to come out on top time and again. The multitalented Brandon Roy

seemed to have this sixth sense. "Basketball is really reacting to situations, and he does a good job of reacting on both ends of the floor," said Blazers coach Nate McMillan. "It's not about just running and shooting and jumping. You have to know how to play the game, and he normally is in the right position." Roy nabbed 2007 NBA Rookie of the Year honors and, with his clutch

play on both ends of the court, entrenched himself as the team's leader—a rarity for a rookie. Roy continued to elevate his game, playing in the All-Star Game in 2008, 2009, and 2010. "You can get more accomplished when you have those guys who understand the game and just play," McMillan said. "Brandon's very versatile."

t has been more than 30 years since the Trail Blazers hoisted their golden NBA championship trophy, but the Blazers have fully reloaded and are today confident of capturing title number two. The first four decades of basketball in Portland have been treasured ones in the Pacific Northwest, highlighted by the brilliant play of greats ranging from Bill Walton to Clyde Drexler. As the team now celebrates its 40th anniversary, Rip City is ready to roll again.

With prized center Greg Oden (below) again sidelined by a knee injury, Jerryd Bayless (opposite) helped pick up the slack in 2009–10.

INDEX